The Little Book of Coaching Success

Foreword by David Clutterbuck

Ben Morton

Copyright © 2014 Ben Morton
All rights reserved.
ISBN: 978-1-291-77208-1

DEDICATION

To Jo and Freya.

My amazing wife and
wonderful daughter.

CONTENTS

	Acknowledgments	vii
	Foreword	ix
	Introduction	xiii
1	Coaching and Leadership; Two Sides Of The Same Coin	Pg 1
2	The Manager Coach Trap	Pg 8
3	It Starts With Me	Pg 12
4	Be Aware Of Your Head Tapes	Pg 19
5	Fair Weather Coaching	Pg 22
6	Get Clear On The Goals	Pg 25
7	Focus On Performance	Pg 28
8	Challenge	Pg 32
9	Coaching Is For Everyone	Pg 35
10	Reaching Elite Performance	Pg 40
11	Be Specific	Pg 43
12	It Goes Both Ways Coaching	Pg 48
13	Be Of Service	Pg 53
14	Be Proactive, Be Flexible	Pg 60
15	The GROW Model	Pg 68
16	Beyond GROW	Pg 74
17	GROW Model Questions	Pg 85

ACKNOWLEDGMENTS

Coaching and leadership are about people and people made this book.
I am hugely grateful to those individuals who gave up an hour or more of their time to talk to me about their experiences of coaching and developing their people. I believe that the book is so much richer for the inclusion of their real life experiences as manager coaches. The case studies are all anonymous and as such the names of these great leaders are not included. You all know who you are and I am extremely grateful for your support – thank you.

This book started with a few power point slides following a spark of inspiration. The finished product is very different and that is a result of two great people fanning the initial spark of an idea.

Firstly, I must thank Richard Nugent for his continual support, guidance, encouragement and coaching. Without him I wouldn't be where I am now and for that I am hugely grateful. I consider it a privilege to call him a colleague and a friend. Thank you.

Secondly, thanks go to Stephanie Walters, another brilliant coach in her own right. She read the initial version of my book when it was a 40-slide e-book written in power point. Her gentle yet direct feedback was the catalyst for turning this book into what it became. I also owe Stephanie a huge debt of gratitude for proof reading and editing my book for no reward.

My personal journey as a coach has been accelerated greatly thanks to time spent working with Dave Reynolds, my coaching supervisor. By skillfully pushing me to reflect more and on a deeper level my skills as a coach have increased dramatically over time. Reflecting on your coaching performance alone can be difficult – Dave helped me to see the wood amongst the trees.

Finally, there are not enough words to thank my amazing wife, Jo. Without knowing it, you have made it possible for me to write this book. You have done this by standing by me, encouraging me and doing all you can to support me whilst starting my business. Whenever I had a 'wobble' you were there to give me a reassuring reality check. You have done all of this whilst leading your own amazing career and looking after our wonderful daughter Freya. Your support has made it all possible.
Writing this book and starting my business has been hard work – and great fun. Jo, you have made it all possible.

Thank you.

FOREWORD

By David Clutterbuck

A few years ago, I gathered the stories of dozens of employees in different organisations about their experience of going on a "line manager as coach course", or when their own manager had been on a similar course. Their stories were depressingly similar, overall. The initial enthusiasm of the course quickly wore off as the reality of coaching in the real world asserted itself. Their direct reports didn't want to be coached, and it wasn't long before a crisis or two impelled the manager back into directive behaviours. Mostly, the direct reports (and the manager) breathed a sigh of relief. When coaching is done in an amateur way, it is clumsy and uncomfortable. And when it is done competently, it is still uncomfortable for the coachee, because it requires them to think and to take greater personal accountability for their own performance and development.

The line manager and his or her team comprise a system and systems theory tells us that changing one part of the system leads the rest to pull it back to how it was before. This was what had happened to these managers. Researchers, such as Stephen Ferrar, have identified a lengthy list of reasons why line manager coaching fails – among them the difficulty of being totally honest in a boss-subordinate relationship and the tendency for hierarchy to push people into parent-child behaviours.

So does that mean that line managers should give up on the idea of being coaches to their teams? Far from it.

Experiments in a variety of organisations, both commercial and educational, suggest that the key is to develop a coaching culture – an environment, where coaching and mentoring are part of the normal tasks and behaviours of the team. Some of the lessons we learned from these experiments include that, to change the team system, it is important that:

- Everyone in the team learns about coaching together (at the same time, over a sufficient period to achieve a change in mindset – this is not about acquiring a skill, it's about developing a collective way of thinking)
- Everyone takes responsibility for both their own learning and everyone else's
- There is a collective team development plan
- The leader supports the team in taking a coaching approach to current and real issues that affect team performance.

With a supportive team behind him or her, the line manager has a much stronger chance of sustaining the momentum of coaching. Equally important, however are two other factors: the support they receive from outside the team and the line manager's own, genuine desire to be a coach (and to be coached).

Support from outside the team comes from a variety of sources. Having a database of further learning materials is helpful, especially if they are on-line. Opportunities to compare notes and co-coach with peers are also effective in maintaining and improving a coaching mindset. Additionally, professional supervision, which is increasingly common in a number of countries, including the UK, can give the coach deeper insight and greater confidence in their ability to support change in other people.

The line manager's internal motivation to learn and to help others to learn seems to be a defining criterion for success as a coach. Among practical things the line manager coach can do to continue to grow in the role are to be coached (and learn from how their own coach works) and to read widely in and around the topics of coaching and mentoring.

Continuous development in the coaching role is essential, both to prevent regression to pre-coaching behaviours and mindsets, but also because the initial skills and approaches taught in coaching courses rapidly become inadequate, when exposed to the reality of day-to-day coaching. Time and again, coaches tell me how liberating it is to learn that they don't have to follow the GROW model — that they have long felt the need to outgrow it. Instead, they gradually accumulate the confidence and the knowledge to relegate GROW to just one of the tools (and often one of the least useful) they can employ in helping a colleague with the quality of their thinking. Like professional external coaches, internal coaches have the opportunity and potential to move through various stages of coach maturity. Doing so has major positive implications for their later career success, because coaching is a critical skill and behaviour that we need from tomorrow's leaders.

The Little Book of Coaching Success positions coaching — and becoming a better coach in the workplace — firmly in the context of continuous self-improvement. It provides insights into what prevents line managers being good coaches and practical advice into how to overcome these obstacles. It makes sure that coaches, who are at the very beginning of their experience, are comfortable with GROW, but then offers guidance and challenge into how to move beyond the relatively simplistic basics and develop their own coaching style. (It's like first learning to ride a bicycle with stabilisers, then abandoning them, when you have confidence and instinctive balance.) Whether you are a beginner as a line manager coach, or one who is looking to enhance their skills, you will at the very least find some useful hints and tips in these pages.

INTRODUCTION

In some ways it is easier to begin by describing what this book is not. The Little Book of Coaching Success is not designed to be a comprehensive 'how-to' guide for coaching. There are so many great books available covering that topic so my intention is not to write another. Nor is this a book designed for those who are totally new to coaching with no prior experience at all.

So what is it and who is it for?

Coaching is becoming more and more prevalent within organisations today. Whilst some organisations employ external coaches, many are training their own. This is a book for all of the internal coaches out there who are quietly going about their work. It is for those managers who believe in the value of investing time in developing their people to achieve great things. It is for the Team Leaders who want to create highly efficient, high performing teams. This is a book for anybody who wants to make coaching 'the way we do things round here.'

In my experience of training coaches and coaching coaches, I have noticed that there are a number of mistakes that manager-coaches often unwittingly make. What's more, I have made most, if not all, of these mistakes myself during my own coaching journey. I've also come to realize that there are some common misconceptions that still exist about what coaching is and what coaching is not.

This book is therefore written with the aim of shining a light on those common mistakes, dispelling the myths and giving you the tools and insights to avoid them. It's a book designed to help accelerate your development as a coach by learning from the mistakes of others. In many ways this book is my attempt to bring to life one of my favorite Chinese proverbs.

> "The wise man learns from his mistakes, the wiser man learns from the mistakes of others."

1 COACHING AND LEADERSHIP. TWO SIDES OF THE SAME COIN

> "Great leaders understand that every team member is unique and every team member adds value."
> Ben Morton

I believe that there is a clear, close and incredibly significant linkage between coaching and leadership. To be a great leader you need to understand how to get the very best levels of performance from your people. To get the very best from your people, you need to know how best to support them, how to coach them.

I also believe that leadership and coaching has never been more important to the success of teams and organisations than it is now. The leadership capability of any team or organisation directly shapes its culture, how innovative its products and services are and the experience its customers have. This direct line between the ability of the organisation's management community to lead, inspire and develop their people is why coaching is now so crucial.

Year on year we see more and more surveys that report the most common reasons why people choose to leave an organisation. One of the most common reasons that consistently appears in the findings is that people leave due to poor management, leadership or a lack of development. How many times have you read or heard this quote?

> "People don't leave bad organisations,
> they leave bad managers."

If there was ever a compelling reason to invest time, energy and resources into developing our ability to support our people then surely this is it. For me, the most effective way for any company to reduce its recruitment costs is to invest money in developing the leadership capability of its managers. It's a simple formula. Better management equals lower staff turnover, equals lower recruitment costs. If you consider the average cost to hire a new starter in 2013 was around £1500 for staff and £4000 for managers, you would at worst break-even on your investment. At best, you would significantly increase performance, improve results and positively impact the bottom line. For anybody trying to build a business case for some form of training investment then surely this must be it.

That may be a compelling business case for the organisation but I often hear managers ask what's in it for them. The answer is a very similar formula to that I described above. Better management equals lower staff turnover, equals less time recruiting and getting new recruits up to speed. It also equals more engaged staff who are willing and able to successfully take on more challenging projects. Ultimately, for you as a manager, the outcome is leading a team that's a pleasure to lead because your people are motivated and successful.

Coaching is happening more and more in organisations today and recent research from the Chartered Institute of Personal and Development shows that:

- Coaching is consistently ranked within the most effective leadership and talent development solutions.
- 45% of organisations plan to utilise coaching to drive organisational performance in the next two years.
- 53% of Private Sector organisations believe their leaders lack the skills to effectively coach their people.

So, for you as a manager this is really saying that coaching your people is one of the most effective things you can do to develop your people. It's also saying that if your organisations isn't already using coaching to improve the business then the chances are that they soon will. Finally, it's telling you that there are lots of managers and leaders out there who don't yet have the skills to effectively coach their people. So this is your opportunity to be one of minority that does.

With this background in mind, I think that it's useful to begin by exploring, just briefly, a few definitions of exactly what we mean when we talk about management, leadership and coaching.

The word *Management* has Anglo-Saxon or Norse roots originating from the word 'Manus', meaning by hand. It is therefore about managing productivity, tasks or resources. For me, management is more about "telling and doing" and less about "showing and inspiring".

Leadership on the other hand has Latin roots meaning 'path' or 'journey'. It's about looking forwards; it's about creating a vision of where you are heading and how things will be in the future. The best leaders have the ability to align people to that vision whilst motivating them to work passionately and relentlessly towards its fulfillment.

Coaching is about helping your employees become more effective, it's about improving their performance and it's about solutions. In this respect coaching is also about the future and their development journey. At its most fundamental level, coaching is about supporting and involving them in the process and investing your time in their development.

Having looked at the definitions we can start to see some similarities and parallels between leadership and coaching. Both are about the future, they are solutions focused, about making things better and moving forwards.

In adopting a management style that embraces coaching, you are becoming a leader. In other words you are helping your people to see their future, to realize their potential and to be inspired by what is possible.

In becoming a manager-coach you are challenging and developing your employees' skills and abilities to achieve the best possible performance results, and to function as self-sufficiently as possible. Yes, it initially feels like more work for you, but you will quickly reap the rewards of the investment you have made in your team. And it *is* an investment – never a cost. They will reward you with hard work, commitment and productivity – what we commonly hear referred to as "engagement".

The "Coaching and Leadership" Story

Organisation: Major British Retailer
Coach: Store Manager
Team Member: All staff in his store…

Interviewing Steven filled me with confidence about the management capability in the UK. The press and industry media can often present less than positive reports about the current status of our management capability and Steven's story is the antidote to that. Having finished interviewing Steven I genuinely felt confident, humbled and inspired. This is Steven's story.

Steven manages a large format retail store working for one of the UK's biggest retailers.

He began by telling me about an individual in his team who was not performing well in their role. The individual was his Stock Control Manager; it was a demanding job that was heavily based around process and routine. Despite struggling with the role he had an incredible work ethic and was a very humble man. Steven said that in his early days as a manager he would have rushed in and tackled the poor performance.

"Seven years ago I would have said that you're not doing a good job, you're taking your pay check so you need to crack on and sort it out."

But that is not what he did on this occasion. Over a period of four weeks he observed the team member and focused on building a sense of rapport with him. This was by just giving him time – 5 minutes here and 10 minutes there. Steven calls this approach Stop-Coach-Go and described the impact that it had on this occasion:

"By using Stop-Coach-Go I was able to get to know him and I found out that he had not been living in the UK for long. He was struggling to adjust to living here as well as struggling with the job. His family and daughter had not yet moved to the country and that was making things even harder for him. I tried to put myself in his shoes and think about how well I would perform in his situation. I absolutely wouldn't and I don't think many people would"

"I took him for lunch so that I could understand his situation and we could work out a way forward. Now that's not something I had time for, in a £1.8 million store you just don't have time for that but it was really important for me to understand what sort of person he was - to give him another opportunity."

"So we gave him another opportunity working on the counters. Because of the connection with me, because I took the time out he was really loyal to me. He really wanted to listen and work with me to understand how we were going to get this tough department performing and how we were going to get them behind him. Being a Stock Control Manager, his role was previously all process whereas counters is about people. It was only through getting to know him that I realized that the person inside wasn't a process person. He was naturally engaging and that is what counters are all about.
I told him that we were on a journey and that I would be with him every step of the way on that journey."

The most powerful thing about Steven's story for me is his approach to leadership. His belief in his people and carving out the time to support them has led to amazing results. Whilst Steven has never been trained as a coach he understands that his role as a manager is to help his team members be more effective and help them to improve their performance. Whilst doing this he was talking about the future, talking about solutions and describing the journey. That is what being a manager-coach is about and in doing so, Steven has become an exceptional leader.

The end of Steven's story is equally as inspiring. Here's how he described it to me:

"Eventually his wife and daughter moved and settled in our country and they have since had another baby. To watch him gain in confidence from the little successes' that we celebrated and shared with the team was amazing.
He now runs one of the best counters in the UK and to see him walking around with Directors because they want to understand and replicate his success is fantastic.
The highlight for me was seeing him when six senior Directors came to visit the counters. He said to me, 'Boss, will you be there?' I said no. This is your time and it's your success – I'll meet them at the door and then it's over to you. I visited the counters in the morning before the visit and the atmosphere was electric."

"After that visit we chatted and I said to him that this wasn't the end of his journey. It was the start of another journey."

2 THE MANAGER COACH TRAP

> "Management is doing things right, leadership
> is doing the right things."
> Peter Drucker

I believe the manager-coach trap is the single biggest challenge for manager-coaches and it is a mistake that so many people unwittingly make. The problem lies in the journey that the vast majority of managers have taken to reach their current position. For most of us, the journey involves being promoted from a functional expert, somebody 'doing the doing', to a manager who now has responsibility for looking after a team of 'doers'. This journey to leadership and management is by no means wrong; it's merely the natural way that most careers unfold and how the majority of organisations fill their management positions. Whilst it's not wrong, it does present a challenge.

If we break down the role of any manager, we can see that there are generally 3 components to the job.

1. Doing 'things'

This is typically what attracted you to your profession or career in the first place. If you're in finance it will be running the numbers, if you're in sales it will be selling, if you're in marketing it will be creating campaigns and so on.

2. Managing 'things'

This involves managing things such as projects, budgets, campaigns or any other resources that you are responsible for. They are the sorts of things that we tend to be given very specific and highly measurable targets for. It is most likely that these are the activities that we will be reviewed against in our annual appraisal and are explicitly linked to the organisations corporate goals or targets in some way.

3. Leading People

This is about inspiring your people, sharing a positive vision for the future, empowering them to act and supporting their growth. It is the activity that we intuitively know can make a significant difference to organizational performance but can often feel intangible and difficult to measure. Whilst there is a great deal of research available that demonstrates the financial benefits of great leadership, many organisations struggle to measure it themselves.

The fact that leading people is at the bottom of this list is the cause of the manager-coach trap. This is why so many people are failing to be the leaders that they could be, the leaders that they are capable of becoming. Very few people, with perhaps the exception of those joining the Armed Forces and one or two other professions, set out in their career wanting to be a leader. For most people it is a bye-product of promotion and this is exactly what creates the danger of the 'manager-coach trap'.

When the pressure is on or when we are stressed, most of us default to a natural prioritisation of our to-do list. This prioritization normally looks something like this:

Firstly, we revert to 'doing things', the things that drew us to our chosen career in the first place. We do this for a number of reasons. One reason is that we like to fall back on activities that are within our comfort zone. Stress is often created out of a lack of 'certainty' about the future which neuroscience now shows to be a critical need for the brain (David Rock; Your Brain at Work, 2009). A lack of certainty creates a strong threat response in the brain activating the same region that lights up during our fight or flight response. Similarly however, rewarding our need for 'certainty' triggers a strong reward response and releases a shot of dopamine, the 'happy hormone'. So, in tackling the tasks that lie well within our comfort zone we provide a short-term stress relief triggered by a short burst of dopamine.

On a similar but more basic level, reverting to 'doing things' allows us to focus on the things that brought us to our chosen profession in the first place. This shifts our focus from our problems, to activities that we enjoy and thus changes our state to a much more positive and productive one. The danger here is that our addiction to the chemical high we get from a quick shot of dopamine means that we can become busy fools. We fall into the trap of investing our time in doing the activities we enjoy and those that we can easily accomplish rather than doing the activities that will give us the greatest pay-off.

Secondly, we focus on 'managing things'. The reason for this is that we tend to be measured on the things that we have to manage. The old adage of 'what gets measured, gets done' really kicks in. Once again, modern neuroscience gives us an insight into what brain activity is driving this behavior. David Rock also identified that we have a fundamental 'Status' need that triggers the exact same response as our certainty need. The thought of failing to deliver upon our objectives generates a threat to our status which we respond to. What will my manager think if I fail to deliver on this? If I don't deliver I may be viewed as less effective than my colleagues? These are the sorts of voices we often hear in our heads that drive and trigger our responses. Whilst the outcome is the same – working hard to deliver – the motivation varies from individual to individual. Some are driven by a strong 'away from' response, they will do what ever it takes not to fail or let somebody down. Some on the other hand are motivated by a towards response – "if I achieve this or over deliver I will be rewarded with a promotion".

Because most of us didn't set out to become leaders, and most organisations don't measure managers against *how* they lead their people, the 'leading people' element of our role goes to the bottom of the 'to-do' list and this is the 'manager-coach trap'. But, the best leaders have learned to flip this natural ordering.

To overcome it we need to get really clear on *why* we are managers and the *type* of leader we want to be. We then have to force ourselves to step off of the hamster wheel and find the time to start thinking, planning and supporting our teams; to be the brilliant leaders, managers and coaches that we are capable of becoming.

So, how do we do it?

3 IT STARTS WITH ME

> "Leadership is the simplest thing in the world because it's just plain you"
> Field Marshall The Viscount Slim

Whilst I absolutely believe that coaching and leadership are not about you as an individual, I do believe that it starts with you.

As leaders, our role is to inspire and motivate those around us. As a coach our role is to quieten our own thinking so that we can give all of our attention to supporting those we are coaching. In either role, leader or coach, we are there to serve those with whom we have the privilege and pleasure to work with.

By looking after ourselves (Me) and managing our own 'state', we can look after and support our teams (Us) so that they can get on and do the 'doing', delivering the objectives (The Results) for the business.

I have introduced this model, or variations of it, in hundreds of training workshops. In every one of these I have asked the participants to think about a typical day or week and estimate the amount of time that they allocate to each of the three elements. The results are always the same. The vast majority of managers spend around 70-80% of their time doing the doing themselves. Sometimes this is even as high as 90 – 95%. At best this leaves between 20-30% of their time to invest in themselves or their teams, which I'd suggest is far too little.

The ideal situation is to hold the three parts, on average, roughly in balance. By managing your time and allocating it between the three elements you are able to hit the sweet spot of leading and coaching.

This equal split of 33.3% of your time being allocated to you, your team and the results is of course somewhat unrealistic. There will be times when the demands of a specific project mean that you need to place a lot more focus on the results yourself – and that is absolute fine. That is the correct thing to do in those circumstances. But, when the work has been delivered or the pressure eases then it is time to redress the balance. You most likely will need to focus on supporting your team again. You will probably also need to focus on yourself and re-charging the batteries.

Consider this familiar situation. It's mid-December and you have been under a lot of pressure at work due to a number of major projects that you need to deliver. You've not had any time off work, other than weekends, since August when you took a one week holiday in the sun. Your partner wanted you to take two weeks off but you said that you were just too busy at work- you really could only take one week. The cumulative effect of this pressure and lack of time off is a build up of cortisol, the stress hormone, in your body. Cortisol's prime purpose is to prepare the human body for action – it controls our fight of flight response and makes us super alert. In order to do this it 'turns off' what it considers to be non-vital bodily processes or functions. One of these is our immune system. We are not designed to have large quantities of cortisol pumping through our veins for protracted periods of time. So, the effect of that pressure at work is a continual drip, drip, drip of cortisol into our body suppressing our immune system. Christmas comes and your body shuts down – you suddenly have the flu, a cold or a sore throat. Why does this always happen you ask yourself? It's because you have not got the balance right.

The first step in getting off the treadmill therefore has to be about getting really clear on where you currently invest your time and then looking to redress the balance. In doing this we start to take back some time, take back control thus enabling us to think, lead and coach our people to the best of our ability.

Some things to try:

- For each of the last five days, consider how much of your time has been spent on activity that focuses on you, your team and the tasks at hand.
- Think about and commit to paper three things that you can *start* doing to change this.
- Think about and commit to paper three things you can *stop* doing to shift the balance.

The "It Starts With Me" Story

Organisation: Major British Retailer
Coach: Store Manager
Team Member: All staff in his store…

This is another story from Steven. Later in the same interview with him I asked how he would describe his management or leadership style. He began by telling me about his "Three C's" – he likes to be Calm, Confident and Caring. However, Steven very quickly told me that he didn't always have this approach. In fact, he said that in the early part of his career he was working too quickly, making decision too rapidly and as a result lost a lot of good people. What was the catalyst for this significant change? Here it is in Steven's own words.

"I've been on a journey. I've been the manager that didn't have time for his people. If I can put it simply, when I became a Store Manager I was just a manager. I could manage anything through process and routine. What I did was move from one process to the next – almost like a Bee.
But then you stop and notice the bodies behind you. At that moment you realise I'm really good at this but I've got nobody with me."

"It really hit home when I moved from one store to another and people said to me "It's been great working for you Steven, but I wouldn't like to do it again."
They said that I was a great manager and they'd learnt so much from me about process and routine. But they also said that it had been so hard and that they were really knackered."

"That made me sit down and think about what I needed to do differently. I realised that I didn't know the people I was working with. At that point I decided that I wanted to start leading people rather than managing them along with processes and routines."

"I now think that management is really easy. But to lead people, you really need to stop and give them time. It could be 10 to 15 minutes, it could be just going and having a cup of tea with them. I like to use Stop – Coach – Go. This is about just taking the time to listen to and help your team members, I really concentrate on listening to the person I'm with. I like to get really clear on how to achieve results and move forward with what it is that the person wants to do themselves."

What struck me from the first few minutes of my conversation with Steven was that his focus was heavily on his people. When describing his current approach to management, he spoke about 'the numbers' or the performance of his store very little. To those unaccustomed with the retail environment this may not seem that significant, but it is hugely significant. As Steven continued to speak it became evident that he had an absolute belief that in looking after himself, he was able to support his people and that would allow him to deliver the results. And deliver the results it did. Here's what Steven said next.

"It's never about the results, the results will happen. So far I've never had bad results in any store that I've worked in. The engagement survey is what's really important and I've never had a bad one of those either."

"I recently took one of my new Operations Managers out

for a cup of coffee, we actually had two coffees and chatted for two hours. Now I haven't got two hours in my day, I just don't. But you can choose to think that way or you can find a way to make the time. I was able to help him see things from a different angle and to support him."

"I normally start any conversation with them, that may be talking about their family, sports that they are interested in or what ever it may be. You are only able to do that if you take time out to get to know them, not to coach them, just to get to know them. This means that later on when you need people to help deliver something - they want to because they feel part of it, because you have that connection."

If there was ever an example of the impact that you can have by looking after yourself so that you can support your team to deliver the results, then this it. Steven's story is all the more remarkable for the fact that he works in the high pressured, numbers driven environment of retail. By slowing down, by focusing on giving time and support to his people he has achieved so much more.

When he looks behind him now, there is a strong team of motivated, happy people who are ready to go the extra mile for him.

4 BE AWARE OF YOUR HEAD TAPES

"Change your thoughts and you change the world."
Norman Vincent Peale

We all have voices in our heads that can sow the seeds of doubt, motivate us to act or cloud our thinking and judgment. The voices in our heads, or mind-talk, are generally developed over a long period of time and are formed based upon our values, life experiences, friends and family.

The problem is not so much that our mind-talk exist, the problem is that we may not always be aware of the impact it is having on our thinking, feelings and actions. Imagine an old music cassette tape that has just one or two songs on it. If you were to play that tape on a continual loop, over and over again, those few songs would eventually be 'stuck' in your mind. You'd be singing or humming the tune to yourself all day long.

Our minds work in a similar way. As a result of our mind-talk we tend to run and repeat a series of 'tapes' in our minds that may or may not be helpful . Either way, these tapes become 'stuck' in our minds driving us towards a specific course of action. This then prevents us from seeing other options or fresh insights.

When manager-coaches observe their team members behaving in problematic ways, they can often find it difficult to talk to them about it. This may be because they are nervous about how their team member may react and that the meeting will turn into a difficult conversation.

The key thing for us to remember is that the 'mental tapes' that we run in our heads are based upon how we *think* the meeting may unfold. It's not necessarily how it *will* unfold.

The problem isn't so much that we run these head tapes in the first place, the problem lies in the fact that we don't rationalize them and take control of our own thought process.

The first step along the road to being confident in tackling these situations is to learn to be aware of the head tapes that we are running. Once we are aware of this internal chatter that is taking place in our minds, we can begin replacing the unhelpful tapes with more productive ones.

Here's an example. An unhelpful head tape may be something like "What if they are upset by the feedback that I share?"

If we are aware of our thinking we could reframe this in a more helpful way, thus replacing the head tape. We might say "I'm providing them with feedback to genuinely help them improve their performance so they shouldn't get upset. Even if they do, they won't be upset for ever."

Some things to try:

- Think of a specific time – a person you need to deal with or conversation you need to have. What was the head-tape that you ran?

- Is that head-tape useful or unhelpful?

- If it is unhelpful - how can you re-frame it?

- Concentrate on and be aware of your own head-tapes. The next time that you catch yourself running an un-useful tape, stop and start playing your more useful, more productive version.

5 FAIR WEATHER COACHING

"A ship is safe in harbor, but that's not what ships are for."
William G.T. Shedd

Fair-weather coaching is in some ways an extension of the manager-coach trap. When the work pressure starts to build, when we're busy or stressed, investing the time in coaching your people can be one of the first things to fall by the wayside. This is understandable but costly for us as leaders, managers and coaches. We now know that a sense of certainty or consistency is something that we need as human beings in order to be in a productive state of mind. If we flip between coaching when things are going well to telling, or at worse doing nothing at all, when things aren't going so well we're removing this sense of certainty. In doing this we not only put our people into an unproductive frame of mind but we also undermine our own credibility as a leader. Your people will not know what to expect from you, the type of leader you are and what you really believe is important.

We looked at some of the reasons that this happens in chapter 2. But why and how else do we let coaching fall off the to-do list?

One reason may be that on a sub-conscious level many managers believe that coaching is distinct and different from doing the "real" work. I passionately believe that it is both an honour and a privilege to lead any team. In accepting the role of a leader, you accept to put your people first, to invest in them and support them. It's not a matter of *then* doing your work - this *is* your work.

Exactly the same is true of coaching. In becoming a manager-coach you are making a commitment to invest in and support your people all of the time, not just when you have time.

Let's consider for a moment how a crisis could be a great coaching opportunity. We know that people learn best when challenged and learn the least when in their comfort or panic zones. But why is this?

When people are in their comfort zone their thinking is not challenged which means that they often complete tasks on autopilot. It's the familiar feeling that we have when we have been driving for several years. You're driving along the motorway and you suddenly catch yourself thinking – "Where did the last ten miles go?"

When people are forced into the panic zone our old friend, the fight or flight response, kicks in once again. It shuts down and diverts resources from many parts of the brain inhibiting learning, insights or creative thinking.

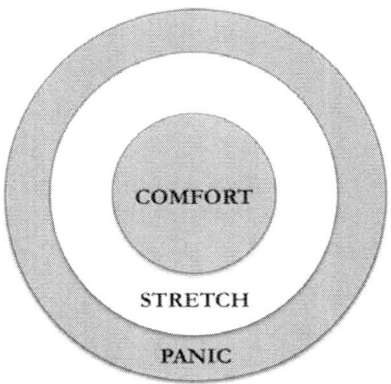

Provided that we give our people the right amount of support, why not use the opportunity to delegate a project to your team member and use it as a fantastic coaching opportunity?

Some things to try:

- Think about the development needs of your team members and the projects that your team needs to complete – can you align the two?

- Think of a team member who is currently in their comfort zone and give them a project that might stretch them.

- Would giving them this project help you as the manager whilst giving them the opportunity to develop?

- Would giving them this project help the team achieve its goals?

6 GET CLEAR ON THE GOALS

"Reach high, for stars lie hidden in you. Dream deep, for every dream precedes the goal."

Rabindranath Tagore

In many ways getting clear on the goals seems an obvious thing to do. However, the biggest shift in my own coaching journey came when I realized just how important and critical this really is. As a time strapped manager or coach it's all too easy for us to pay just fleeting attention to this before we start jumping into problem solving or solutions mode. This isn't necessarily a bad thing so long as we have properly identified and understood the goals.

Let's look at an example. At some stage in our coaching career most of us will have experienced a session that goes something like this.

You're 15 minutes into the coaching session and your team member seems to be jumping from one topic to the next. Your head starts spinning and the chatter in your head is going into over-drive. You hear voices in your head saying things like… "I don't know what to say next," I'm not sure

I can help," "Oh no, I didn't hear what he just said because I was thinking about what to say myself," "I'm really not sure what he needs right now?"

I certainly recall a session like this when I first started coaching. In fact, I remember a number of sessions like this.

The way to overcome this situation is to get really clear on the goals for the session at the beginning of the meeting. If you're working with an individual for a period of time then it's worth investing time in understanding their overall goals for the coaching relationship. Be prepared for the fact that it might take up an entire hour-long session to really identify and then breakdown the goals.

I once asked a client what their goal for our coaching relationship was and they told me "I want to be a better leader." That was it. They didn't tell me anything else at all. If we had just merrily skipped onto the 'Reality' phase of the GROW model, or any other model to that matter, I have no doubt that we both would have become lost in a rambling coaching conversation. Instead of diving straight in we spent a great deal of time exploring in what ways she wanted to be a better leader, in what situations, with what types of people? What was working well for her, what wasn't working so well? What data, evidence or feedback did she have that told her she needed to improve?

Identifying and understanding the real goal can often require more of you as the coach than simply asking what they want to achieve. You will sometimes need to coach their objectives out of them by means of a series of great questions. You may also need to set realistic expectations of what can be achieved in the time that you have. Getting crystal clear on the outcomes means that you can always steer the session back to the goal and keep things on track as required. This is even more important during the very first session and for the manager-coach. In having this important conversation about their goals for the coaching relationship you may get some unexpected insights from someone who you assumed didn't really "need" coaching.

Some things to try:

- Consider identifying the goals as a mini coaching session in its own right.
- However much time you have spent in the past identifying the goals with your team member – double it next time and see what impact it has.
- When you think you are clear on the goal, pause, think and then ask some more great, clarifying questions.

Some questions to ask:

- What do you really want to do?
- What would success look / sound / feel like?
- When do you want / need to achieve it by?
- What do you really want from a career / job?
- Why is this important to you?
- What would be ten times better than that?
- What do you want from this session?
- We have x minutes today, what would be the most useful things for you to achieve?
- If a miracle happened overnight and the challenge went away, how would you know? What would be different?

7 FOCUS ON PERFORMANCE

"Don't lower your expectations to meet your performance. Raise your level of performance to meet your expectations. Expect the best of yourself, and then do what is necessary to make it a reality."
Ralph Marston

Performance is perhaps one of the most misunderstood terms in business today. I would also suggest that it is unlikely that you will find one common definition of performance within any one organisation. Try this experiment. Ask any ten managers or leaders in your organisation for their definition of performance and see how many different responses you get. I'm guessing it will be ten, perhaps nine at best.

If your organisation is similar to the majority, I suspect that many of your performance definitions will actually be describing results or outcomes. For example, if you ask a sales team leader about their team's performance you'll likely here things such as; 'we've sold 50% of this week's target so far and it's only Tuesday' or "we're 20% off our target for the week'. This isn't describing performance.

This is describing the results or the outputs. The danger with this misunderstanding of performance is that we begin to obsess over the outputs and they become our sole focus. In doing so, we miss the opportunity to get really clear on the components or ingredients that *enable* performance. Yes, your team member may have delivered the goal but if you don't focus on performance you'll miss the fact that they could have done it faster, better, easier, more cheaply, more collaboratively etc., etc.

So, here's an alternative definition for you to consider.

"Performance is about doing the things that need to be done in order to achieve the results you desire."

Performance is therefore about getting really clear on the activity that needs to take place in order to enable you to achieve the results you want. But it goes further than that. Performance is about seeking out improvements and making everything you do better so that you are generating the conditions for success. At its best, performance is about identifying what's working well so that you can replicate it over and over again.

Notice that the focus here is on what's going well and on solutions. Far too many personal development plans and annual performance reviews focus on what we need to rectify or be better at. In other words, they are problem focused. The challenge with this is that we leave these performance reviews being an expert in our own failings. We are acutely aware of everything that we are not doing well and everything that is not working for us. And here's the key thing - the results we see in life are a result of where we put our focus. So what impact is this likely to have on us?

Consider achieving peak performance as trying to complete a puzzle whose pieces have been hidden around your house. In order to complete the puzzle you must first find all of the pieces. In this respect your role as a manager-coach is to help your team members identify all of the things that work well for them. In doing so, they can approach their challenges from a position of strength and positivity as opposed to a position of weakness. Once you have done this, then you can focus on developing each strength and making each part better and better until you reach the point whereby success is almost guaranteed.

Some things to try:

- Get really clear on the goal and then identify the performance factors that must be present to achieve the outcomes.

- When discussing objectives and personal development plans try asking your team member how they can use their strengths to achieve their goals.

Some questions to ask:

- What's working well for you right now?
- What has worked for you in the past in similar situations?
- How could you do more of that?
- How can you ensure that you do that more consistently?
- What else can you do that will have a positive impact upon your results?
- How will you know if it is working or not – what feedback or signs will you see?
- When reviewing successful outcomes consider asking 'What could you have done differently to achieve the same outcomes more quickly or easily?"

8 CHALLENGE

"Happiness is not the absence of problems; it's the ability to deal with them."
Steve Maraboli

Many managers new to coaching unwittingly make the mistake of thinking it's about teaching people how to do it.

In our busy, time-poor working environment it can be all too easy for managers to approach a 'coaching' session by asking their team member what they think and then suggesting how they would have tackled the problem themselves. In doing so, they then conclude that they have successfully coached their team member.

But this isn't coaching. Whilst this approach may enable your team member to quickly complete the task at hand, it is a short-term approach. The danger of this approach is that your team members begin to rely upon you for the answers to all of their challenges. You may have heard managers saying things like 'why can't my team members think for themselves' or 'why do they always come to me for the answers'; you may even have uttered those words yourself. The reality of this situation is often not that team members 'can't think for themselves'; it is that they have learned not to think for themselves. Why? Because as busy, time strapped managers we tell our team members what to do or how we tackled similar challenges in the past. In this respect you are conditioning your team members to respond in the same way as Pavlov did with his dogs. It is like Pavlov asking, "Why do they come running every time they hear a bell?"

If this is your default management style then it is also likely to result in your team approaching their work with fairly low levels of engagement. As a result they may feel unfulfilled at work because they have little scope to solve their own problems and think creatively. To deny a person the opportunity to solve their own problem fundamentally misses what it is to be human. Our ability to solve problems and think creatively is what separates us from every other species on the planet.

The alternative approach is to coach your team members. This is about building another person's own ability to act and enabling them to identify their own solutions. Yes, sometimes a person may need a new technical skill, which is something that we can teach or show them. Whilst this is an extremely valuable way of developing our people, it isn't coaching either.

More often than not, a person needs help thinking through and solving a work challenge on their own, or identifying the thoughts or behaviors that are limiting their performance. This kind of help requires you to ask carefully considered questions, not to tell them what to do.

Here's a key insight. As a coach, manager or leader it's not your job to provide all of the answers. In fact, the sooner that you realize and accept this, the sooner you'll become a great coach, manager and leader.

It's not your job to work hard in providing the answers. It's your job to work hard in challenging the person being coached so that they can find their own answers.

The real learning happens when you help the team member to surface their own answers and this is when lasting changes are created.

Some questions to ask:

- What options do you have?
- What else could you do?
- What would the worlds leading expert in 'x' do?
- What are the pros and cons of each option?
- Would you like another suggestion?

9 COACHING IS FOR EVERYONE

> "Leadership is unlocking people's potential to become better."
> Bill Bradley

It is a common misconception amongst many managers who are new to coaching that it's just for those who are underperforming in some way. This is absolutely not the case. In adopting this mindset, we are immediately denying many in our teams of the opportunity to excel, to grow and to perform at the level they are capable of reaching.

If we look at the history of coaching we find that it has its roots in elite sports performance. How many sports coaches do you see or know of who work with athletes who are consistently under-performing? The answer is none or very few. Professional sports coaches work with hugely talented individuals and focus on moving their performance from good to great or from great to world class.

If this is the case – why would we confine our coaching skills to just our under performers?

Everybody in our teams and organisations, irrespective of their current performance level, is on a development journey. Regardless of where they are on this journey they have the potential to make significant performance improvements with the right coaching and support.

Your highest potential team members and your top performers will have their own challenges and development needs. Think about the challenges that these team members might be struggling to overcome. Career growth; a desire to broaden their impact in the organisation; a frustrating working relationship; moving from being a team member to a manager.

Their challenges are equally as important and equally challenging for them. Helping them to find their own solutions can have as significant an impact on the organisation as raising the performance of those with performance challenges.

There is another huge benefit to coaching your high potentials. As a group within the organisation these individuals can often be those who have the highest likelihood of going to work for your competitors. Why? Because they tend to be hugely ambitious, with a desire to progress upwards through the company. The challenge with this is that there are fewer positions for you to promote them into. Without careful management and support, this group of your most talented people can become frustrated and seek opportunities elsewhere.

I once heard a story that in trying to tackle high staff turnover MacDonald's famously posed a different and slightly unusual question. They asked themselves 'what would we need to do to make our people want to leave the organisation?' From this question they discussed and created a world-class learning and development plan that they then implemented. What happened? Staff turnover plummeted. Their people felt so supported, valued and invested in that they no longer wanted to leave – they wanted to continue working for a great company.

So, if you invest the time in coaching all of your team, you will be rewarded with greater engagement, loyalty, a hunger for improvement and much faster development.

Some things to try:

- Set aside one hour to coach all of your team, individually, every two weeks. This should be solely about their goals and their agenda. It's not a session to discuss your needs or daily business tasks.

- Think about the possible challenges that all of you team may be facing or wrestling with?

- Think about the challenges you faced when you were in your team members' shoes?

The "Coaching is for Everyone" Story

Organisation: Major UK Bank
Coach: Senior Manager
Team Member: Manager

Alice was a Senior Manager within a major Bank's Head Quarters who needed to recruit for a new senior team member. Following a number of changes to her team's structure and responsibilities her instinct was to look externally for the new team member rather than promoting from within. Alice was working with a coach herself at the time and during one session she described her goal as this:

"I'm recruiting for a new senior team member and have decided that I am going to go with an external candidate. I would like to talk about how I can keep the two internal candidates motivated when they find out that they are not getting the role."

As the coach explored the goal and the reality of the current situation with Alice, several interesting things came to light. Firstly, she had interviewed the external candidates but she had not yet interviewed the two internal candidates. Secondly, she had not listed the pros and cons of recruiting internally versus externally.

The outcomes of that coaching session shifted Alice's thinking entirely. The key insight for her was the realization that coaching was not just for her underperformers. It was also for her top performers and those in new roles.

Having carefully considered the benefits and concerns of both options (and deferring her decision until she had completed all of the interviews) she realized a number of things. The internal candidates had 90% of the skills and experience needed in the new role but her major concern was the time it would take them to 'get up to speed' in the new role. Interestingly, she also realized that the external candidates had the required technical expertise but lacked the knowledge of the Bank, its culture and ways of working. What this meant for Alice was that she would have to devote the same amount of time to supporting the external candidate, possibly even more time, than she would developing the internal candidate. At the same time as supporting them, she would have to work hard at maintaining the motivation of the two disappointed internal candidates – her original goal.

Alice's breakthrough came from the realisation that coaching is a powerful tool for everyone and not just her top performers. She also came to understand that spending time coaching her team members really was an investment and not a cost.

10 REACHING ELITE PERFORMANCE

"When you're through learning, you're through"
Will Rogers

There are a number of things that separate the 'elite performers' from the 'average performers'. I think that one of the most significant factors is the hunger for learning, development and insights that elite performers have.

When the majority of us are learning a new skill, our hunger for learning decreases with the passage of time. Learning to cook is a great example. In the beginning as we learn to cook we start with the basics. We don't try and to be too adventurous and we perhaps don't know what is possible, we don't know what we don't know. As our skills grow we may take it up as a more serious hobby. Our hunger to learn grows, we may start to watch cookery programmes, read books and magazines, go on courses and experiment. Then, as time passes and we find that we can make a pretty good go of making most things from our favorite cookery books, our appetite for learning begins to tapers off.

This is the point at which the distinction is drawn between the elite performers and the average performers, as shown in graph below.

Sticking with the cooking analogy lets think about some of the worlds' greatest chefs. The likes of Heston Blumenthal and Michael Roux Junior immediately spring to mind. There is something very special and distinct that has enabled them to reach and maintain their level of mastery. It is the fact that their hunger for knowledge, insight and development remains as high with the passage of time as when they first set eyes on a pan.

As a result they continue to seek opportunities for growth, learning and perhaps more importantly, feedback. The most dangerous point in any individual's development is when they think they have nothing left to learn.

It is for this very reason that I believe you should focus as much time and effort on coaching your high-potentials as those with performance challenges. Perhaps your coaching sessions with your high potentials may focus around helping them to identify where the next 1% improvement may come from.

Some questions to ask:

- What is the worlds leading expert in your field doing right now?
- What else could you do to take your performance from good to great?
- If you were to observe yourself for a full day, what performance insights or feedback would you share with yourself?
- In a year's time, when you are on stage receiving the award for being the best at "X", what will you attribute your success to?

11 BE SPECIFIC

"Feedback is the breakfast of champions."
Ken Blanchard

One of the biggest mistakes that managers often make when giving feedback or conducting appraisals with their team members is not being specific enough. Not only does vague feedback deny the individual of the information they need to improve their performance, it also activates a strong status and certainty threat. By providing vague, unspecific feedback you immediately trigger your team member's mind talk. This begins a spiral of events where key parts of the brain are 'turned off' limiting creative thinking and fresh insights.

The ability to share detailed feedback in a productive, non-threatening manner is critically important for manager-coaches. But why does it sometimes feel so challenging to provide detailed, feedback?

Whilst coaching, I have found that there is generally one of two things at the heart of this challenge.

It may be that the manager-coach is genuinely unable to precisely identify the challenge or performance gap that needs to be addressed. Or, it may be as a result of the 'head-tapes' that they are running and concerns about how the feedback may be received.

Whatever the root cause, the outcome tends to be the same. The way that many manager-coaches tackle this challenge is either by being very vague with the feedback that they provide or by avoiding giving the feedback altogether.

So what they actually do is say things like this...

"You need to be more of a team player," or "You need to think more about the bigger picture".

Feedback to a team member can be tremendously valuable, especially in helping to raise the team member's awareness of a potential blind spot. But useful feedback must be carefully delivered whilst requiring accurate descriptions of observed behaviours and their effects.

For those unaccustomed to receiving feedback it can often feel threatening and personal. When this state is triggered the individual is unlikely to respond positively to the feedback. One of the simplest ways that I have learned to position feedback in a non threatening way is to begin with the words 'For me...' The reason that this is so effective is because the feedback is positioned firmly as your thoughts as opposed to a statement of fact. Consider these two ways of delivering the same feedback.

- A. "The opening of you presentation was not impactful enough"
- B. "For me, I thought that you could have opened your presentation with more impact."

In these two examples the exact same feedback has been communicated but it has been communicated in very different ways. I know which of the two I would respond more positively to and which those that I lead and coach would respond more positively to.

Another simple, yet hugely effective method for providing feedback is the 'three points of contact' tool. Imagine a coaching or feedback session where there are three elements present; you represent one element and your team member is the second. The third element or 'point of contact' is a document that contains the details or facts relating to the performance feedback you are trying to communicate. This might be a record of the individual's time keeping, sales results, customer service feedback or whatever data you have relating to their performance. Having started the conversation and began by building some rapport the technique is used in the following way. Have the document to hand and say something like this; "John, I'd like us to have a conversation about your latest customer service results which I have a copy of here." As you say "here", place the document onto a table between the two of you. This technique works by placing the focus of the conversation not on either of you (thus making it non personal) but onto the document containing the facts. Continuing by saying something like "I'd like us to work together to find a way of improving these scores" further positions the feedback in a positive and solutions focused light.

Both of these methods of providing feedback are designed to help your team member remain in a positive and resourceful state. By using these tools they are able to listen to the feedback without feeling threatened which in turn allows them to use it productively.

I have described how feedback must be both carefully delivered as well as being specific and accurate. As a manager-coach, it's important to discipline yourself to look for those specific, observable behaviours before you provide your feedback. The key here really is in sharing observable and specific data. One of the skills of a great coach is to remain impartial and not to make judgments about your team member, their situation or actions. As human beings we are by nature meaning-making creatures. This means that when we observe specific behaviours we naturally make assumptions and inferences about what it is that we have seen. These assumption and inferences are largely based upon our own personal experiences, values and beliefs, which means that they may or may not be accurate. So, the skill and discipline really is in observing the specifics and feeding this back to our team members without making any judgments. For the manager-coach this can be a real challenge as the impact of your team member's actions will often have an impact on you, on the rest of your team and on the things that you are responsible for.

There is no easy answer to the challenge though. It requires self-discipline, and a genuine belief in the benefits of coaching for you to invest your time in the coaching conversations.

Some things to try:

- Frame you feedback by saying – "Can I share some observations with you?" or "Would you like me to share some observations."

- If you are not able to provide feedback immediately, make a note of specifically what it was you observed. Then find the earliest opportunity to share the feedback.

- Try using WWW.EBI. **W**hat **W**orked **W**ell was… it could have been **E**ven **B**etter **I**f…

- Trying beginning feedback with "For me…"

- Try using 'Three Points of Contact" next time you need to provide some feedback.

12 IT GOES BOTH WAYS

"It is literally true that you can succeed best and quickest by helping others to succeed."

Napoleon Hill

A common mistake for new manager-coaches is to treat coaching as a one-way exchange.

In the early days of coaching there can be a lot of new information to make sense of and even more to try and use in your initial coaching sessions. Or at least it can feel that way.

It's no surprise therefore that many manager-coaches start out assuming that the learning, and feedback, in a coaching relationship flows in one direction – from you to your team member.

This misunderstanding denies you of the opportunity to develop and grow. In the process of your coaching relationship, you have the chance to profoundly grow and develop. If you fully commit to coaching then you will be transforming yourself from a command and control manager (who manages through process and routine as

Steven once did) into a supportive leader, enabling and inspiring others to act.

In doing so, you'll find fulfillment through enabling and seeing the growth of those around you in service of a collective goal. You won't just be focusing on what your people achieve; you'll be focusing on how they achieve it. You'll be focusing on performance and not just results, you'll be focusing on the things that great leaders focus on.

One of the most effective ways of developing your skills as a coach is to work with a coach yourself. Those working as professional coaches often refer to this person as a 'coaching supervisor'. Unfortunately, the term 'coaching supervisor' often seems to have some negative connotations attached to it. The reason I'm sharing this with you now is that I do not want you to believe or accept these negative connotations. I have met many coaches who feel that they can't possibly work with or admit to working with a coaching supervisor. The fear is that in admitting they have a coaching supervisor it suggests that they are not an expert; that they are not perfect.

I have a coaching supervisor. I'm not an expert and I'm not perfect. I do however focus on my performance and I am serious about continuing to develop so that I can be the best coach I can possibly be.

For me, it feels somewhat incongruent to not work with a coaching supervisor. How can we ask our team member's to focus on and reflect upon their performance if we do not do this ourselves? This isn't a sign of weakness; it is a sign of great strength that gives so many positive messages.

As a coach it says 'I believe in coaching', 'I'm serious about performance' and 'I want to keep developing so that I can support you'.

As a leader it says 'I'm authentic', 'I'm comfortable in sharing my development needs' and 'I don't necessarily have all the answers and I'm cool with that.'

I began my career in the British Army at the age of 16. At 15 I met with a Major from the Army Recruiting Team whose job was to prepare me for a two-day assessment centre. Something he said has stayed with me throughout my entire career, both in and out of the Army. It has also helped me in my journey as a coach. This is what he said.

> "Ben, remember that as a leader you do not need to have all of the answers."

I think that this is absolutely true of a leader and manager. In fact, I strongly believe that the sooner you come to realise and accept this point the sooner you'll become the leader you are capable of becoming.

At the age of 22, I arrived at the Regiment I had been posted to as a young Second Lieutenant ready to take command of my Troop of soldiers. Those 'under my command' consisted of a Troop Sergeant (with 15+ years experience), three Corporals (each with 7+ years experience), three Lance Corporals (each with 5+ years of experience) and 18 private soldiers some of whom also had in excess of 5 years experience. I could have took command by virtue of my rank, believing that I was 'in charge' and that they would follow me because that's what the hierarchy says they should do. This wasn't what I did although I saw a number of young officers unsuccessfully take this approach. I wanted my Troop of soldiers to willingly follow me and to respect me as a leader – not just the rank that I wore on my shoulders. The way that I achieved this was by always remembering that I did not have all of the ideas. I drew upon the vast amount of experience in the troop. We planned together and in doing so a huge amount of trust grew amongst us. Admitting and accepting that I didn't have all of the answers didn't undermine me as leader; it made me so much stronger.

Whilst I think that it is important as a leader to understand that you do not need to have all of the answers, I think that it is even more significant for you as a coach. For coaches I believe the same statement should read as follows:

"Remember that as a coach, you absolutely do not need to have all of the answers."

In summary, I believe that as coaches we must be open to learning and feedback ourselves. We should regularly reflect on our performance, seek feedback and work with a coaching supervisor. As a manager-coach working in an organisation this could well be another manager-coach. It's likely that you will have a network of peers and colleagues who are having similar coaching conversations. What a great source of knowledge sharing and learning these people could be!

Some things to try:

- Find a colleague with whom you can discuss your coaching performance with at least 4 times a year.

- Make time to reflect upon your coaching sessions and write down your reflections.

- Ask your team members for feedback.

Some questions to ask:

- Could I have done anything better to support you?

- What could I have done to make this session even more valuable for you?

- Do you have any feedback for me as a coach that would like to share?

- If you were in my shoes, what would you have asked you that would have been really valuable?

13 BE OF SERVICE

"Serve to Lead"

Motto of the Royal Military Academy Sandhurst

One of the most significant and costly mistakes you can make as a manager-coach is neglecting to ask the person being coached how you can be most helpful to them. This is also one of the most powerful, yet most overlooked questions that a manager-coach can ask their team members. For example, when did you last ask this question?

"What can I do to really help you right now?"

One of the best coaches, trainers and facilitators I have had the privilege to work with is hugely skilled at understanding and un-covering the outcomes that the person he is coaching is looking for. Here are just a few of his brilliant opening questions.

- "What would make this session really valuable for you?"
- "What can I do to make today an 11 out of 10? What would be the cherry on top of the cake for you?"
- "What would make this coaching session outstandingly valuable for you?

You need to be aware that as a manager-coach you have a particular challenge and potential pitfall that does not exist for external coaches. That is the challenge of failing to be of total service to your team member or of hijacking their agenda. As a manager-coach you absolutely must approach your sessions with a great deal of clarity and integrity. It is not uncommon for manager-coaches to find that their interests and those of their team members are in conflict. For example, your team member may be trying to clarify and understand their long-term career goals, whilst at the same time you may clearly see them as a successor for your position.

As a manager and a coach, you need to remain aware of this potential for conflict and the danger of steering the outcomes in a direction that meets your needs. This means that you need to provide clarity about which "hat" you are wearing at any particular time. Your role as a managerial coach is not to impose your will on your team member in the guise of coaching.

Providing Feedback

Whilst your job as a coach is absolutely to support your people, it is also your job to provide them with performance insights and feedback that they cannot see for themselves or that others are perhaps not prepared to give. This can be a real challenge in the early stages of our coaching journey because giving feedback is something that many managers feel a little uncomfortable doing.

We generally tend to feel less confident undertaking new activities or in new situations because they feel unfamiliar to us. By committing to giving more feedback, the very thing that makes us feel uncomfortable, we are able to expand our comfort zone. It will not instantly make giving feedback the most comfortable thing in the world (although it may for some), but over time, by consistently doing it we are able to expand our comfort zone.

I'd like you to try a very brief experiment for which you'll need both arms. Once you've read this next paragraph you'll need to either prop the book up so that you can continue reading or alternatively, put it down altogether and spend a few moments reflecting on your management and coaching style. So, here's what I'd like to you do. Firstly, I'd like you to simply fold your arms. Once you have done that, I'd like you to fold them the other way so that the opposite arm is on top. You probably had to think carefully about this and it probably now feels a little awkward or uncomfortable. The reason that it feels awkward is because it is not something that we do very often. Now, keep your arms folded in that position and either continue reading this chapter or spend a few minutes reflecting on your coaching style.

If you still have your arms crossed, the chances are that you have forgotten that it ever felt uncomfortable. The reason for this is that over time, our comfort zone expands to include those activities that once felt uncomfortable. This is exactly what will happen to us and our team members when we start to offer and receive feedback more frequently. Feedback will become the norm and norms are those things that we are inherently comfortable with.

There is one other amazing benefit in adopting a coaching management style. Your team members will start to expect, want and ask for feedback from you. In coaching your team members and offering feedback you not only expand your comfort zone, you expand theirs too. This creates a virtuous circle where giving feedback leads your team to seek out feedback making the process easier and easier for all involved. Feedback ceases to be something that they receive twice a year as part of the appraisal process and becomes just the way you do things.

Having invested the time and effort in developing your coaching skills, it's not surprising that your focus can, at times, be on how you are doing as a coach. In the early days of my coaching journey I would often find myself listening to my own mind-talk during a session. I'd be listening to a voice in my head saying things like 'what model should I try and use next?', 'what question should I ask next?', 'how am I doing right now?' or 'am I any good at coaching?'

But here's the thing that I eventually realized. That's the exact opposite of what I should actually have been doing.

The very best coaches, the truly world-class coaches, put all of their energy into helping the person being coached to become great. They focus fully on their team member and put all of their effort into listening to what they are saying which creates a virtuous circle. By listening and watching intently, they hear, see and feel exactly what is being said. This is in turn means that they do not need to worry about what questions to ask as the questions become obvious, they just seem to appear in their minds.

In focusing more on our team members and less on ourselves we are being of genuine service to them. In doing so we will became great coaches. The time to reflect upon our own performance is after the coaching session, not during in it.

Some things to try:

- Be of service by giving full control of planning the agenda for one to one meetings to your team members.
- Before giving some feedback ask your team member "Can I share an observation with you?"
- Look for opportunities to give more feedback – it will strengthen your 'feedback muscle'.
- Create a safe, regular forum in team meetings where your team can provide each other, and you, with feedback.

The "Conflicting Priorities" Story

Organisation: Major Travel Company

Coach: Sales Director

Team Member: Sales Team Leader

John, a Sales Director, in a travel company was about to leave his organisation after many years service. As a consequence of his departure, a Joint Venture project with another company in the Group would be unlikely to continue unless a very talented member of his team, Sarah, moved to the other company.

Several months prior to John's departure, Sarah came to him asking for advice about whether she should take the role in the other company or not. John said that at the start of his management journey he would have immediately given advice and suggestions of what to do, based upon the fact that it was advice that Sarah was asking for.

However, in this case, John moved into coaching mode and began asking a number of great questions such as 'Why is this a difficult question for you?', 'What are your concerns?' and 'What are the things that you're thinking about?'.

John's main aim was to help Sarah arrive at her own solution that she felt confident about committing to.

During the course of the coaching conversation it became clear to Sarah (and John) that the move to the other

organization would not be the right thing for her. The consequence of this realization was that Sarah would ultimately leave her current company as her job would cease to exist.

It was at this point that John became conscious of his conflicting priorities as a manager-coach. On the one hand he believed in supporting and looking after his team so supporting Sarah's decision felt right. On the other hand, despite leaving the organization he had a great deal of loyalty to the company and Sarah's departure would have an impact upon them.

John's final decision was ultimately bourn out of his beliefs and values. To quote John, he said "By that point I'd got to the position where I was very much in the belief that if you know there is somebody who is no longer motivated by the job they are doing, there is no point in trying to talk them into staying in that role. You're better off helping them to go where they need to be and finding someone else for that role."

14 BE PROACTIVE, BE FLEXIBLE

> "Be infinitely flexible and constantly amazed."
> Jason Kravitz

As a manager-coach you have the unique opportunity to be pro-active and not rely solely on your team member to identify their needs and initiate the coaching conversations.

As we have already discussed a number of times, it's important to be responsive to your team member's needs and not to drive the agenda yourself but that doesn't mean that you can't be pro-active when the opportunity arises.

As a manager-coach you have the opportunity to see your team member in their working environment which is an advantage you have over external coaches. This allows you to observe their performance and provide focused, developmental feedback. So, if you are conscious of this, on the occasions when they arrive at your one to ones with 'nothing to discuss' you can suggest topics based upon what you know of them and their performance.

At this point it is worth reflecting once again on the most common route to management that we explored in Chapter 2. That is the journey from being a 'doer' or functional expert, to a team leader, then manager, senior manager, director and beyond. This journey means that it's highly likely that you will have experienced very similar, if not the same, challenges that those in your team are facing. It's also highly likely that you may know some of the challenges that they will face before they do. Your team member may not know when they are facing a particular challenge, heading for a landmine, or about to make a big mistake – but you probably will. So, it's important that you remain pro-active and ready to spot trouble on the horizon.

This unique position that you can find yourself in as a manager-coach presents the danger of you driving the agenda. However, it also presents a fantastic opportunity for you to serve those that you lead. For the expert manager-coach this is about moving seamlessly between coaching and mentoring. It is about flexing your style and utilizing your skills as both a coach and mentor. But what are the differences between coaching and mentoring?

Coaching is characterized by a partnership approach whereby the coach asks questions of the coachee and in doing so, challenges their thinking to enable them to arrive at their own solutions. In this respect, a coach doesn't necessarily need to have experience of the coachee's work, environment or specific challenges.

In contrast, a mentor will share their specific experiences of tackling challenges that are similar, or perhaps the same, as those facing the mentee. A Mentor will share their experience, advice and learning of similar situations in order to help the mentee develop. Another notable distinction between the two is that coaches' focus on providing support and encouragement whereas a Mentor will focus on providing specific advice. So what does this mean in practice?

On the occasions when your team member comes to a meeting with nothing to talk about, or at least nothing that they have prepared in advance, you are in a great position to support them. The key coaching skill of being able to use inquiry to surface what's going on for them at that moment, whilst drawing on your own experience to identify un-recognized challenges is incredibly powerful.

In these situations it really is the blend of coaching and mentoring coupled with a collaborative mindset that creates the conditions for success. As a manager-coach it's important to resist the temptation to switch into 'tell' mode and assume that the way *you* tackled a situation, is the best way or the only way. By highlighting the challenges, sharing some of your experiences and continuing to coach you can achieve some amazing results. This approach can often lead to some truly innovative ideas and break through solutions for them, for your team and for your business.

In summary, being proactive can appear, on the surface at least, to be the opposite of 'Being of Service'. But in reality, it is not that clear cut. Whilst it's extremely valuable to prepare for any coaching session, and I would always encourage you to do this no matter how experienced you are, it's also vitally important that you remain flexible.

Entering the session with a view on the kind of conversation that you want or could have does not mean that you are failing to be of service or hi-jacking the agenda. But once you get in the room, your main job is to really listen to and understand your team member. Your job is to help them tackle the challenges that they are facing whilst still being ready to point out the unknown. In doing this, you really will be of service to them. In doing this you really will be a leader.

Some things to try:

- Set aside time before a coaching sessions to think back to when you were doing the job, or a similar job, to your team member and ask yourself these questions:
  - What were the mistakes I made that I could have avoided?
  - What do I wish I knew then?
  - What were the challenges that I didn't see coming?
  - What did I muddle through that could have been better?
  - What would I like to have had another shot at with the power of hindsight?
  - What do I know about the organisation or sector that they don't that will be of value to them?
- Ask yourself what experience, insight, observation or piece of feedback you have that would be valuable to share?
- Consider what you need to do, if anything, to stay in coaching mode and out of 'tell' mode.

The "Be Proactive, Be Flexible" Story

Organisation: UK Retailer
Coach: Commercial Director
Team Member: Commercial Manager

David, a Commercial Director, in a large UK retailer described his approach and philosophy to managing and leading the people within his team like this:

"I think that people are much more willing to work for you, to achieve and be focused on doing a good job if they feel happy in their surroundings; if they feel happy with where they are in that moment in life. Someone who spends their time constantly thinking about whether or not they are doing a good job, where their next career move is and whether or not the current role is the right one for them is not going to be focused on delivering in the role. I think that if they feel that they are being developed and have an idea of where they are going they are much more likely to perform. Having an idea about where they are going is not just about moving on or being promoted. That is not everybody's aspiration and for those people it is about affirmation that they are still developing and doing a great job. I think that my job as a leader is to create an environment where this can happen and carve out the time to support my people. If you lose touch of that then you can lose touch with them, what's important for them and what they are doing."

From the very beginning of my interview with David it became apparent to me that he has a very proactive approach to leading and developing his team. On several occasions he used phrases like 'carve out time' and 'creating an environment where they can develop.' The next question that I asked David was how does he go about doing this?

"I make sure that I spend at least one hour per week with each of the people that I have reporting into me. We don't always use all of the time, it depends very much on the individual, but I ensure that I create the space regardless. I don't intend for that time to be used to discuss their objectives, the tasks in hand or what's going on in work. It can be about that but it doesn't have to be – I certainly do not put any restrictions on the agenda. If they want to talk about personal development, career plans or even how they are feeling in that moment – all of those are fine with me. I like to be led by what they want to do."

David went on to share a fantastic example of how he proactively prepares for these one to one meetings whilst balancing a coaching and mentoring style. He described a time when he had somebody working for him, Sarah, who just wasn't happy working in the culture and environment of the organisation. It wasn't a case that she wasn't good at her job, because she was. Equally it wasn't about those around Sarah giving her a hard time, because they weren't. It was more the case that she couldn't understand how others were working in the organisation and they couldn't understand her. Because of Sarah's personality it came out almost as a moan when she was describing her situation. This is how David described the situation, what he did and the outcome his actions created.

"It almost got to the stage where every week I would sit and listen to Sarah moan. But I did sit and listen every week because I felt it was the right thing to do and it enabled her to get it off of her chest. I waited every week until she had finished and then stopped. I then said lets take it a step back. The first thing I did was to make it really clear that I had listened to what she said and that I understood how Sarah was feeling so she felt supported. I absolutely think that is part of my role – to be there and support my people. The second thing I would do is to reflect back what I had heard along with my understanding of what she had said. Then, the third thing I did was to share what I would have done in her situation or how I would have tackled the same challenge. I was trying to recommend a way that she could get around the problems she was having with certain people and the organisation's culture."

"But I knew from fairly early on that I could sit there and do that every week but Sarah just really wasn't comfortable in the culture of our organisation. It just wasn't her and what we were talking about every week were the symptoms of that. So, as time went on I started to prepare more in advance for our meetings and began adding a fourth element to the discussion. I would say that we had tried everything I knew and yet we were still having challenges. So, I asked her to really think about what it was that she wanted. For me it felt like Sarah wasn't happy in the role and I wanted to share my observations with her and for her to understand that I recognized that. We discussed the fact that I wanted to do something to support her but within the framework that I had, I wasn't sure if I could offer her the solution she wanted or needed."

"At the end of the day, we came out of that situation. There was no break down in the relationship, she was happy and able to continue working for me and we got the best out of the situation. The real outcome was that as a result of our sessions she came to the point in her own mind where she said 'ok – I've had enough' and she went and got a great job elsewhere, outside of the organisation. The great thing for me is that we have stayed friends after that, in fact we went to a festival together with some of her ex-colleagues too and we all had a great time. So I was pleased in that respect that we maintained a good relationship and got the best out of something that was never going to work."

There are so many great things that we can take away from David's experiences of coaching and mentoring Sarah. The first is his blend of coaching and mentoring – by using the coaching skills of questioning and active listening he was able to understand her situation, but perhaps more importantly, demonstrate to Sarah that he understood her situation. In doing so he showed a great sense of empathy that helped Sarah to feel supported within the team despite her frustrations. Whilst utilizing his coaching skills to understand her situation he then gave suggestions based upon his knowledge and experience of the organisation. In doing so, he blended the skills of a coach and a mentor to great effect.

There is another great lesson hidden in David's story. That is the skill in identifying the goals and also the confidence to not be afraid of revisiting them. You will recall how his approach changed over time – specifically when he mentioned the fact that they had tried everything he knew, how it still wasn't working and that he wanted Sarah to really think about what it was that she wanted. This is an example of a great coach re-clarifying the goal.

In this fantastic case study we have heard how David focused on his team member, took a pro-active approach, re-focused Sarah on her goals whilst the whole time was being of service to his team member.

15 THE GROW MODEL

> "A coach is part advisor, part sounding board, part cheerleader, part manager and part strategist."
>
> The Business Journal

The GROW model is perhaps one of the most widely used coaching models within organisations and by coaches in the early part of their coaching career. Its success, I believe, is partly due to its simplicity and versatility. In the early stage of a manager-coaches career I believe that the model provides a simple, yet powerful structure to base your conversations around. GROW stands for:

- **G**oal

- Current **R**eality

- **O**ptions (or Obstacles)

- **W**ill (or Way Forward)

Establishing the goal is about working with you team member to identify the behaviour or situation that you want to change. In doing so, it is important to identify a clear goal. If you have done this well, you should both have a clear idea of how you will be able to tell if the goal has been achieved.

The next step is to explore the "Reality" by asking your team member to describe their current situation. This is an important step as all too often people try to solve a problem without fully understanding their starting point. Imagine how difficult it would be trying to plan a journey in your car if you did not know where you were starting from? Trying to achieve a goal without understanding the reality, or current situation is exactly the same. It's often the case that the solution, or the keys to the solution, are hidden amongst the current reality.

Once your team members have explored the current reality, or the start point, then it is time to explore the "Options" for achieving the goal. This is about discussing all of the possible options and asking your team member 'what else' to help them identify other possibilities that they may not have considered without your support. Once you have identified all of the options, your task moves on to helping them identify which options are most suitable for them.

The final step in the process is about discussing the "Will" and helping them to commit to the actions that you have discussed. Having a clear goal and even a plan to achieve it isn't always enough to make change happen. This final step is about helping you team member to commit to the actions that you have discussed. It may be by discussing what you or others can do to help, it may be about clearing obstacles or it may be about recognizing and celebrating success along the way.

I said that discussing the "Will" was the final step but that's not strictly true. Whilst the model normally starts with the Goal and ends with Will – it doesn't have to a model that you follow linearly. At any stage of the model you may well find yourself moving backwards as you seek to re-clarify or check the goals. Similarly, you may find yourselves suddenly fast forwarding to "Will" because the mere process of discussing the goal or reality has made the obvious next steps appear. Whilst the GROW model provides a framework and set of steps to follow, you should not allow it to drive the coaching conversation. The model is a tool to enable great conversations, not a process to be rigidly adhered to. It really is the conversation that is important and not the model.

Whilst I have given a brief overview of the model, my aim is not to provide you with a step by step guide for coaching with GROW. I have however included an insightful case study that shares one coach's personal journey of practice and discovery using the model. As with the other chapters in this book, I hope that this will help to accelerate your development as a manager-coach.

This section is also includes a collection of great coaching questions that I have used during my own coaching journey. Hopefully, some of them will be of use early in your coaching career. Hopefully they will prompt your thinking and enable you to develop your own bank of powerful coaching questions. But perhaps more significantly, I hope that they inspire you to start coaching your people and in doing so, help you to become the leader you are capable of being and becoming.

The "GROW Model" Story

Organisation: Major Telecoms Company
Coach: Training Manager
Team Member: Customer Service Operator

I started coaching back in my days as a trainer in a large Call Centre. I was expected to be a great coach and to help staff improve their performance. The trouble was that my experience of coaching had been limited to the sports world – where coaching meant that the coach demonstrated a technique, had the person try it out and then tell them what they did wrong in order to correct it. I was sure that coaching in a business context couldn't be the same, could it?

Around that time, I experienced a 2-day coaching skills programme – teaching me the GROW model, some listening skills and, of course, the feedback sandwich. I was released out on to the call centre floor to listen in on calls and provide coaching to those lucky advisors whose customer interactions I had monitored.

I tried to follow GROW as my trainer had taught me, and the session often went something like this:

Coach: "What's your goal for this session?"

Advisor: "errr... for you to tell me how I have done whilst you've been listening in"

Coach: "Hmmmm... OK. How do you think the call went?"

Advisor: "Fine, I think"

Coach: "Good. Good. What are the opportunities for you to improve next time?"

Advisor: "Look – what the hell are you on about? Just tell me if I did OK or not"

Then I would give them a feedback sandwich...

"Well, I thought the opening was really nice – and you closed it well. You gave the customer lots of incorrect information though. However, your voice sounded really professional"

Of course, I wasn't always this bad – and over time I developed my rapport skills and ability to give feedback in a way that added value for the advisors, and ultimately for the customers.

So, there is a place for really great performance feedback, and for coaching on the intricacies of a specific process. It forms the meat and drink for many people in business today and the chances are that your journey as a manager-coach started with the GROW model in a similar way to me. However, this was just the beginning of my coaching journey.

Many years after ditching GROW, I finally saw it applied the way I'm sure it was meant to be. I worked with a coach whose opening question was "How can I help?" They moved elegantly through the stages of the model, jumping back and forth as the client required, drawing from a huge bank of high quality questions.

They created new resources in the clients they worked with, helping them to explore new options before helping them to decide on the most congruent option and then encouraging the client towards absolute commitment to action. Most impressive of all was that the coaching was 'content-free'. They never once advised or led – she simply asked great questions.

16 BEYOND GROW

> "To know oneself is to study oneself in action with another person."
> Bruce Lee

Whilst I believe that the GROW model is a fantastic tool for any coach to use at the beginning of their career, I also believe that it's important to master it and move on. But let me be clear. When I say move on, I do not mean abandon the model all together. Here is what I really mean.

As a leader, I believe that I have always led and managed my teams with a style akin to coaching. In the early part of my career this was due to the belief I had in those I was privileged enough to lead. It certainly wasn't due to a conscious awareness of what coaching was and its benefits. At that time I believed my team had great ideas and were capable of achieving amazing results with just a little support from me. I also fundamentally believed, and still do, that I did not have a monopoly on great ideas –

remember the Major from the Army Recruiting Team in Chapter 12?

Many years later having left the Army and found myself leading a HR Function within a large travel company I became conscious that coaching existed as a development tool. I did some internet-based research and read a dusty copy of "Coaching for Dummies" that one of my team found in the back of a cupboard (I'm not sure if she was subtly trying to tell me something back then?). At this point I rather clumsily started to experiment with and use the GROW model to coach and mentor colleagues in my team and the organisation. Reflecting back on those early attempts to use the model the experiences that my team members had was not dissimilar to those described in the GROW model case study. I rigidly moved my team members through the various steps of the model feeling pleased that we had arrived at the 'Will' stage with some commitments in place.

Sometime later I realised that the model wasn't working that well for me, or those whom I was coaching. At this point I decided to ditch the model and go back to what I had intuitively always done.

The Development Coach

As with the coach in the last case study, a long time after giving up on GROW, I finally saw it being expertly used. I watched a number of coaches skillfully use the model as a supporting framework. They seamlessly moved backward and forwards through the model in a manner that was designed to do nothing else other than help the person they were coaching. Because they were comfortable with the model they were able to focus intently on the individual that they were coaching. This in turn meant that they were able to ask the right questions at the right time that would best help their clients. They helped them identify new solutions and possible approaches that they had not previously considered. Finally, they explored these options in a manner that enabled the individual being coached to commit to those actions which best suited them, and most significantly, those that they could commit to. This was much more than simply arriving at "Will" and testing their commitment as I had done in the past. But perhaps most impressive of all was that the coaching was 'content-free'. They never once advised or led – they simply asked great questions.

Some years later, whilst completing a coaching course myself, I finally mastered the GROW model and felt really comfortable using it. When I say mastered it, I actually mean several things. Firstly, I understood the model and had embedded it into my subconscious thinking. Secondly, I understood that it was a framework to support a session and not a strict methodology to be followed linearly to control the session. Thirdly, and perhaps most significantly, I understood that it was one of many coaching tools that I could blend together as the circumstances required. To this day I still find that the most powerful of those other tools is ability to focus on the person I am coaching and listen intently.

I learned that my new-found coaching persona was often given the label of "Development Coach". Great developmental coaches spend more time focused on what their client is saying (or not saying) than to the coaching model itself. They are masters at matching and mirroring – and perhaps most important of all – they help their clients to focus on what is possible – not just what the problem is.

As my colleague Richard Nugent once said, in this second phase of evolution, the emphasis is on development. When he discovered that coaching didn't just have to be remedial – his fire was well and truly lit. At that point he was certain that he wanted to be a coach. But what he didn't yet appreciate were the possibilities that still lay ahead when he fully developed the new skills he was acquiring.

The Master Coach

The next phase in the life cycle or evolution of a coach is that to Master Coach. If your approach to leadership, developing yourself and your team encompasses several of the points below, then you are probably a master coach already.

- You know the fastest single way to build deep rapport with your team members.

- You have an extensive bank of great coaching questions to draw upon – but more often that not, the most elegant resource-unlocking question just pops into you head intuitively.

- You are a master of your own emotional state and are able to strongly influence that of your team members.

- You are able to help your team members create outstanding performance breakthroughs even when you are not the expert, or even experienced in, the challenge that they are facing.

- You draw on the work of great coaches and transformational coaches such as Nancy Kline, Michael Neill, David Clutterbuck, Sir John Whitmore and other valuable sources such as the Solutions Focus and Flow.

Whilst your focus as a master coach is still firmly on respecting your team members map of the world – and not suggesting or leading them down any particular route – you can help them to commit more fully. When I first arrived at this point in my coaching journey I naively thought that coaching wasn't about the models, it was just about listening and asking great questions. I went as far as to argue the case for abandoning the models and suggesting that new coaches should just focus on listening to their team members. My belief was that in doing so, the right questions would just 'appear' in your mind. But let me state this next point quite clearly.

I was totally wrong.

To get here takes dedication, practice, study and commitment. I only reached the point at which those great coaching questions 'appeared' because I had spent time using the models, practicing and most importantly, reflecting on my own coaching practice. The models are an important, no - a vital, part of the evolution of a coach. Abandon them completely at your peril.

All that said, if you are at the point of being a Master Manager-Coach, I believe that you are already making the work-place and the world a better place.

The "Master-Coach" Story

Organisation: Central Government Department
Coach: Senior Civil Servant
Team Member: All of his team

James is a senior manager within one of the major central government functions. Unlike many of those interviewed for the case studies in this book, he has received some formal training as a coach along with an extended period of reflective coaching practice. This is how James described his coaching journey and his approach to leading his department.

"I think that I have always had a management style that encompasses coaching, even before I had any formal training as a coach. Having now trained as a coach though it is now even more obvious to me that this is a far better way of managing the team, the work and achieving the outcomes. A coaching approach to management creates a real sense of 'buy-in' from the team and it also allows me to take a more appropriate view of the work across our portfolio. I do not need to be in the detail of what all of my team are doing - they have the expertise and experience for that. Coaching has allowed me to have more of an overview of the work in our portfolio, ensure that the right links are made across the department and to support individuals development. As a result of applying my coaching skills I'm now finding that my team are resolving many issues themselves. I physically see their faces light up when they realise they have solved their own challenges, there is much more of an acceptance of responsibility yet at the same time they feel like there is a weight that has been lifted off of their shoulders. I think that this is due to them having the freedom to make their own decisions, balanced by support from me and the confidence that they can solve their own problems."

James has clearly been on a significant journey as a coach and it was interesting to hear him say that it is now obvious that coaching is a much better way to manage. Earlier in this book I described how in adopting a coaching style it can initially feel like more work for you as the leader. I think that James' story is proof of the value that coaching brings in the medium to long term. We heard from James how his team now largely solve their own challenges, how much more engaged they are with a greater sense of buy-in and their willingness to accept responsibility. What manager would not want a team with those skills and attitudes?

James also shared with me a little of his journey beyond GROW and towards becoming a Master Coach. Here's what he said:

"As a result of my coaching training and having logged in excess of 100 hours reflective coaching practice I find that I use the various tools on much more of an unconscious level. I don't consciously think about the models that I am using or even about using them in a structured way. It is only by reflecting on my coaching sessions that I became aware of the fact that I am blending different tools together, at different times, in order to achieve the outcomes for my team member. Whilst I'm using the tools less consciously in the session, I am now much more conscious of reflecting on my own skills and thinking about how I can improve."

"The other significant change, which affects all that I do, is that I am now far more aware of the questions that I ask and how I ask them."

"The final thing that I would also say is that I am now far less concerned about whether I am coaching or mentoring. Whilst I am always clear about which 'hat' I'm wearing at any point in time, I'm happy to move between the two and find a balance between coaching and mentoring. Whether I'm coaching or mentoring is less important to me now so long as I am helping the individual to move forwards and achieve their outcomes."

The Transformational Coach

A Transformational Coach will do whatever is necessary to help their team member or client create what they want to create. Often this starts by helping them to understand the power of 'creating'. If you are new to this distinction between 'reporting' and 'creating' the closest single phrase I'd use to sum it up is the one credited to Kathlyn Hendricks:

> "Your life is a reflection of what you are already committed to."

Transformational Coaches have a deep understanding of just what is possible. They realise that, when you are swimming in the sea, it's hard to see the water – so often the most transformational work is the most obvious. In this respect they are focusing 100% on the individual, not themselves, their ego or calling themselves a coach. Another distinction is that they work best when their team members are ready to be coached.

This is the point at which Leader and Coach become one and the same. The two-sided coin that I referred to in the opening chapter of this book has been fully forged. They realise that as a great manager-coach or leader, they exist to be of service to those that they lead. The transformational coach uses metaphor, stories and their own life experiences on top of their already honed master coaching skills to help their team members realise their full potential.

To reach this point they have also become totally comfortable with who they are as a leader. They do not hold back in fear that their team members become more successful than they are. They do not recruit team members who are 'B players' for fear or being upstaged.

Their goal is to help all of their team members reach their full potential, for themselves and for the organisation. If this means that their team members achieve more than they do themselves - then they see that as a sign of their own success as a leader.

The final thing that they realise is that they can learn just as much from their team members as their team members learn from them; it goes both ways.

The Next Level

I'd like to end with an admission. I don't know what the next stage of the development of a coach or manager-coach is. In fact, I don't have a clue. What I do know is that there is another level. I'm not there yet, but I'm working hard to get there. Sharing my thoughts with you in this book is part of my journey and I'm looking forward to finding out where it will take me.

The most important thing about this for me is that I'm comfortable not knowing and I'm comfortable telling you that I don't know. And here's why:

"Ben, remember that as a leader you do not need to have all of the answers."

The Army Recruiting Major

Goal Questions

- What do you really want to do?
- What would success look / sound / feel like?
- When do you want / need to achieve it by?
- What do you really want from a career / job?
- Why is this important to you?
- What would be ten times better than that?
- What do you want from this session?
- We have x minutes today, what would be the most useful things for you to achieve?
- What would be your ideal outcome?
- What is your future perfect scenario?
- How will you know if this session has been useful to you?
- What would need to happen for you to leave this session feeling that it was outstandingly valuable?
- How can I be of most help to you today?

Reality Questions

- What's happening now?
- What exactly do you mean by …?
- When you say…, what exactly do you mean?
- How often do you face this challenge?
- What's your current situation?
- Who else is involved?
- Tell me the three most important things about the issue?
- What have you done so far? How successful has this been?
- What results have you achieved so far?
- What's helping?
- What's getting in the way?
- What are the obstacles you find yourself facing?
- What's missing in this situation?
- What is really going on?
- What are you not telling me?
- What's holding you back?

Options Questions

- What options do you have?
- Tell me 3 things you could do?
- What else could you do?
- What would the worlds leading expert in x do?
- What if (time, resources etc) were not an issue?
- What are the pros and cons of each option?
- Would you like another suggestion?
- If it didn't matter if you failed, what would you do?
- Have you experienced a similar challenge before? If so, what did you do then that worked?
- If you took just one tiny action, what would it be?
- What's currently working for you that you could do more of?
- Is there anything that you could stop doing that would have a positive impact?

Will Questions

- What are you going to do next? By when?

- Will this get you the outcome you want? If not, what else will?

- What barriers or obstacles might you face and how will you overcome these?

- Who else needs to know about / support your plans?

- What support do you need? (think about resources, people etc)

- What could I do to support you?

- What commitment on a scale of 1-10 do you have to taking the agreed actions?

- What would move you 1 point further up this scale?

- What prevents this being a 10?

- What would you need to do to make this a 10?

- What could you do to increase your commitment?

- To what extent has this session achieved the outcomes we set?

ABOUT THE AUTHOR

Ben Morton is an international team development consultant and coach whose clients range from small and solo business owners to FTSE 100 companies and international brands.

He is a Chartered Member of the CIPD (Chartered Institute of Personnel and Development) with approaching two decades of experience in leadership, learning and management. His broad range of experience is gained from roles including Group Head of HR and Training for a global subsidiary of TUI Travel and more recently 2-years in the Global Leadership Training Academy at Tesco.

He began his career in the British Army and trained at the Royal Military Academy Sandhurst. Ben completed two operational tours of Iraq, initially as a Platoon Commander and again as an Operations Officer leading 180 soldiers before resigning his Commission as a Captain in 2006.

As a consultant at TwentyOne Leadership, Ben specialises in two key areas. Firstly, he works with clients to enable them to understand what is required to develop high performing, highly effective teams. Secondly, he helps individuals moving into their first leadership role or those whose careers have progressed rapidly, finding themselves leading large and often very experienced teams.

Bibliography

Paul Z Jackson and Mark McKergrow, *The Solutions Focus,* Nicholas Brealey International, 2007

David Rock, *Your Brain at Work,* Harper Collins, 2009

Michael Neil, *Supercoach,* Hay House UK, 2013

Nancy Kline, *Time to Think,* Cassell, 2002

Simon Sinek, *Leaders Eat Last,* Portfolio Penguin, 2014

David Megginson and David Clutterbuck, *Techniques for Coaching and Mentoring,* Routledge, 2004

Susan David, David Clutterbuck and David Megginson, *Beyond Goals,* Gower, 2013

John Whitmore, *Coaching for Performance,* Nicholas Brealey Publishing, 2004

Mihaly Csikszentmihalyi, *Flow: The Psychology of Happiness: The Classic Work on How to Achieve Happiness,* Rider, 2002

Notes

Printed in Great Britain
by Amazon.co.uk, Ltd.,
Marston Gate.